Primary Numbers

A New Hampshire Number Book

Written by Marie Harris and Illustrated by Karen Busch Holman

Photo reference for the number 20 provided by Canobie Lakes Park through the photography of Karen Holman. Used with permission.

Thanks to Charter, the poets of Skimmilk Farm, and to the unfailingly game Karen Holman. —*M.H*

Many thanks to family, friends and neighbors for all their help and support and a special thanks to Marie Harris for her words, guidance and friendship. —*K.H.*

And to the wonderful people at Sleeping Bear.

—Marie & Karen

Sleeping Bear Press
310 North Main Street, Suite 300
Chelsea, MI 48118
www.sleepingbearpress.com

THOMSON
———✦———™
GALE

© 2004 Thomson Gale, a part of the Thomson Corporation.

Thomson, Star Logo and Sleeping Bear Press are trademarks and Gale is a registered trademark used herein under license.

Printed and bound in the United States.

10 9 8 7 6 5 4 3 2

Library of Congress Cataloging-in-Publication Data

Harris, Marie.
Primary numbers : a New Hampshire number book / by Marie Harris ; illustrated by Karen Busch Holman.
p. cm.
ISBN 1-58536-192-5
1. New Hampshire—Juvenile literature. 2. Counting—Juvenile literature.
I. Busch Holman, Karen, 1960- II. Title.
F34.3.H375 2004
974.2—dc22   2004006092

The New England Sled Dog Club hosts the oldest continuous sled dog races in the northeast. They take place in Tamworth, New Hampshire beginning in January. One-dog sleds are raced in the junior category by girls and boys aged five through nine. Could one of them be you?

Many Alaskan malamute and Siberian husky champions were born at the Chinook Kennels, founded in Tamworth in 1930. Some were on the teams that accompanied Admiral Byrd to the Antarctic. Others were used by the Army for search and rescue missions.

There was a man from New Hampshire famous for making dogsleds. His name was Ed Moody. Today his apprentice, Jeff Johnson, carries on his tradition in Bartlett.

Do you know why this book is called *Primary Numbers*? New Hampshire holds the "first-in-the-nation" presidential primary.

one

1

1 husky pulling
    one speedy sled.
One junior musher
    races ahead.

There are moose in the woodlands all over the northern parts of the world. What makes the moose special in New Hampshire is that it helps our state's natural resources. How? By having its picture on special license plates, which raises money for all kinds of conservation projects such as planting native wildflowers along roadsides, restoring the Common Loon to the state's lakes and ponds, and repairing the historic Fort Constitution in New Castle.

The New Hampshire Fish and Game Department has a bumper sticker that says BRAKE FOR MOOSE IT COULD SAVE YOUR LIFE. That's because moose often wander onto roads and highways and drivers need to be very careful not to hit them.

Moose are the largest animals in the deer family. They can grow as tall as 7 feet and weigh as much as 1,500 pounds. Moose are herbivores, which means they like to eat trees and shrubs. The word "moose" comes from the Natik word meaning "the animal that strips the bark off of trees." The hoofprint of a moose is shaped like a heart.

two

2

2 moose in north woods
deep in the snow
nibble on spruce shoots
by the moon's glow.

The Port of Portsmouth—up the Piscataqua River three miles from the sea—is one of the oldest working ports in the country. In the seventeenth, eighteenth, and nineteenth centuries, wooden ships of all descriptions loaded and unloaded cargo and traded their wares up and down the Piscataqua River and the smaller rivers that flow into it: the Cocheco, the Oyster River, the Lamprey, the Bellamy, the Salmon Falls, and the Squamscott.

In the old days, ships sailed out of Portsmouth to ports along the Atlantic coast and all over the world carrying fish, lumber, bricks, and many products from New Hampshire. And ships brought manufactured goods to our shores from Europe, things a new country would need like books, special tools, and clothing.

Today the Moran Towing Company's fleet of tugboats escorts oil and gas tankers and other huge vessels loaded with gypsum, coal, and salt. And certain tugs can be equipped with special fenders to help move nuclear submarines safely in and out of their berths at the Portsmouth Naval Shipyard.

three

3

3 sturdy tugboats
ready to go.
There's a big tanker
needing a tow.

The brook trout is our state's official freshwater fish. It has lots of nicknames: squaretail, speckled trout, brookie. Brook trout are very beautiful. Their iridescent bodies are blue or green and speckled with yellow spots. They live in cold rivers and streams, lakes, and ponds.

Fishermen—sometimes called anglers—love to fish for trout. They use all kinds of artificial flies, made to look like the real insects trout like to eat. Some popular ones are the stone fly, the case caddis, the black gnat, the mayfly, and the hornberg, which imitates a terrestrial insect that lives by the Isinglass River. Anglers try to "match the hatch," which is a way of saying that they tie or buy flies that copy how each insect looks when it hatches out and lands on the water.

Opening day of trout season is the fourth Saturday in April.

New Hampshire has many kinds of fresh and saltwater fish. A good place to learn more about them is at the Amoskeag Fishways in Manchester.

four

4

4 wily brook trout
hunting for flies.
Which are the real bugs?
Which ones are tied?

5 fiddlers bowing
tunes for the dance.
Shall we learn new steps?
This is our chance!

Country dancing—sometimes called "contra dance"—comes to New Hampshire from all over the world, including England, Ireland, Scotland, and Canada. The music for these dances can be played by one fiddler or a whole orchestra of fiddles, guitars, banjos, autoharps, harmonicas, accordions, and lots of other instruments.

The Canterbury Country Dance Orchestra is one of New Hampshire's oldest contra dance orchestras. When you come to a dance, you don't have to know all the steps...the "caller" will teach you. Everyone, young and old, has fun at a barn dance!

Marcel Robidas grew up listening to the music of his Franco-American heritage. He began playing the fiddle when he was a young boy. He always wanted to make his own fiddles, but his farm chores took up most of his free time. Years later, in Dover, he began to repair fiddles, and finally built his first one in 1982 when he was more than 50 years old. He is now a master fiddle maker and he still performs at concerts and dances all over New England.

five
5

6 loons are calling
at the lake's edge.
Some sit on nests made
of twigs, mud, and sedge.

Fishermen used to put sinkers made of lead on their fishing lines to help weigh them down. Too often loons swallowed those sinkers and died from lead poisoning. But today loons in New Hampshire and all over the country are safer because our state was the first to ban the use of lead sinkers. Now fishermen use sinkers made of a wildlife-safe element, called bismuth, instead.

On a very big lake, like Lake Winnepesaukee, there could be more than one pair of nesting loons. Loons build their nests close to the water. They are made from whatever materials are available—pine needles, grass, leaves, moss, sedge—held together with mud from the lake bottom. Eggs are usually laid in June. When the chicks are grown, they fly to the sea and they don't come back to the place they were hatched until they are three or four years old and ready to lay their own eggs.

Once you have heard a loon's voice, you will never forget the sound!

six

6

The Cog Railway was the first of its kind in the world. Completed to the summit of Mount Washington in 1869, trains run on two rails laid on a wooden trestle. The locomotives and coaches are equipped with cogs that engage the rack in the center of the tracks.

The locomotives are powered by coal-fired steam engines. Every train has an engineer, a fireman, and a brakeman. Now take another look. See! The locomotive is *pushing* the coach up the mountain. And on the way down, the seats in the coach are turned around and the engine coasts on its own—it's not even connected to the coach—while the coach brakes do most of the work.

The Cog Railway was built to bring tourists to the top of the mountain, and that's what it still does today. A museum at Marshfield Station features a full-sized locomotive cab and lots of pictures and artifacts from the old days.

seven
7

7 steam engines
push cars up the track.
They climb tooth by tooth
moved by cogs on a rack.

MOUNT JOHN QUINCY ADAMS

MOUNT JEFFERSON

MOUNT MONROE

MOUNT ADAMS

8 mountains named for
eight presidents.
Climb the White Mountains
with backpacks and tents.

MOUNT WASHINGTON

MOUNT PIERCE

MOUNT MADISON

MOUNT EISENHOWER

The Presidential Range is in the White Mountains. One of New Hampshire's nicknames is "The White Mountain State." Mt. Washington is the highest peak east of the Mississippi River. It is part of the Presidential Range which forms a 12-mile-long ridgeline of mountains named for U.S. presidents: Madison (5,363 ft), Adams (5,798 ft), John Quincy Adams (5,410 ft), Jefferson (5,715 ft), Washington (6,288 ft), Monroe (5,385 ft), Eisenhower (4,761 ft), Pierce (5,385 ft).

Recently, the New Hampshire legislature agreed to change the name of Mt. Clay (5,533 ft) to Mt Reagan in honor of Ronald Reagan, our 40th president.

Hikers like to climb these mountains, though sometimes the changeable weather can make climbing dangerous ...even in the summer!

The Old Man of the Mountain—thousands of years old and New Hampshire's state symbol since 1945—crumbled off Cannon Mountain sometime in the middle of the night on May 3, 2003.

eight

8

The first "after-supper" amateur baseball league in the country was founded in 1909 in Concord, New Hampshire. It was called the Sunset League. Play began after supper (6 p.m.) and continued until sunset. The original teams were the Haymakers, Old Timers, Sluggers, and White Parks. Players from the Sunset League went on to careers in the major leagues. Perhaps the most famous of them all was third baseman Red Rolfe, who played for the New York Yankees from 1931 till 1940 alongside Babe Ruth and Joe DiMaggio. His team won five World Championships! The league exists to this day.

In 1946 the New England League Dodgers, a Nashua team, was one of the first integrated teams in organized baseball. Roy Campanella and Don Newcombe led Nashua to a league championship.

New Hampshire has been home to almost 50 major league players. Today the state has a pro team called the Nashua Pride, which is part of the Atlantic League.

nine

9

3rd Baseman

Shortstop

Outfielder

9 baseball players
bat in the park.
Come watch the game and
stay until dark.

10 glowing pumpkins
too scary to eat.
These jack o' lanterns
grin "Trick or Treat!"

At the Keene Pumpkin Festival you can take hayrides, pumpkin-mobile rides, fire engine rides. You can put on a costume and march in a parade. There are fireworks and all kinds of food. But best of all, you can see the jack o' lanterns. Every October, on the Saturday before Halloween, people carve thousands and thousands of pumpkins...so many that the festival is in the *Guinness Book of World Records* for the largest number of lit jack o' lanterns at one time in the world. A new record was set in 2003... 28,952 lit jack o' lanterns!

Come to the festival! And bring your pumpkin to add to the count. Maybe this year you can help set another world record!

ten
10

11 mild Holsteins
walk toward the barn.
Time for the milking
here on the farm.

The Tuttle Farm in Dover, established in 1632, is the oldest continuously operated family farm in America.

The New Hampshire Farm Museum in Milton is comprised of the Jones Farm (listed on the National Register of Historic Places) and the Plummer Homestead.

The Farm Museum hosts all kinds of activities to show how life was lived in the old days. You can learn to milk a cow and make butter, cheese, and ice cream. You can watch oxen plow a field, learn to build a stone wall, watch how cider is made, and even go on a hayride! Exploring the Farm Museum makes you feel like you have traveled backward in time.

eleven
11

12 Shaker boxes,
stacked up by size,
just right for storing
treasures inside.

Ann Lee came to America in 1774, bringing with her a new religion called Shakerism (they got their name from the whirling and shaking they often did when saying prayers). Mother Ann and her followers were looking for a place to practice their religion in freedom and peace.

Shakers were simple, hardworking people who lived in their own communities. There were once 19 Shaker villages in America. One of them was in Canterbury, New Hampshire. Today, you can visit and see where they once lived and worked.

Shakers were always looking for ways to make their work easier and they came up with many good ideas for the kitchen, the laundry, the garden, the barn, and the infirmary. They made beautiful furniture and other wooden items such as oval boxes that "nest" inside one another.

Shakers shared their good ideas with everyone for free. We still use many Shaker inventions like the clothespin, the circular saw, and the flat broom.

twelve
12

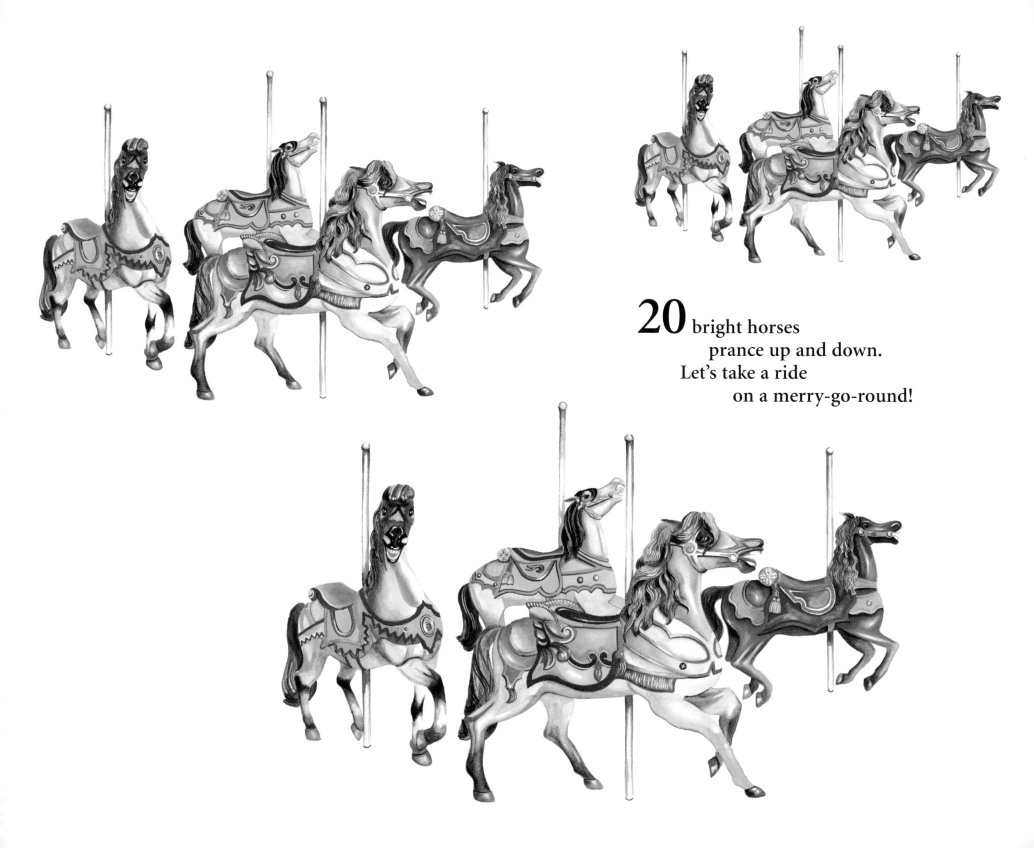

20 bright horses
prance up and down.
Let's take a ride
on a merry-go-round!

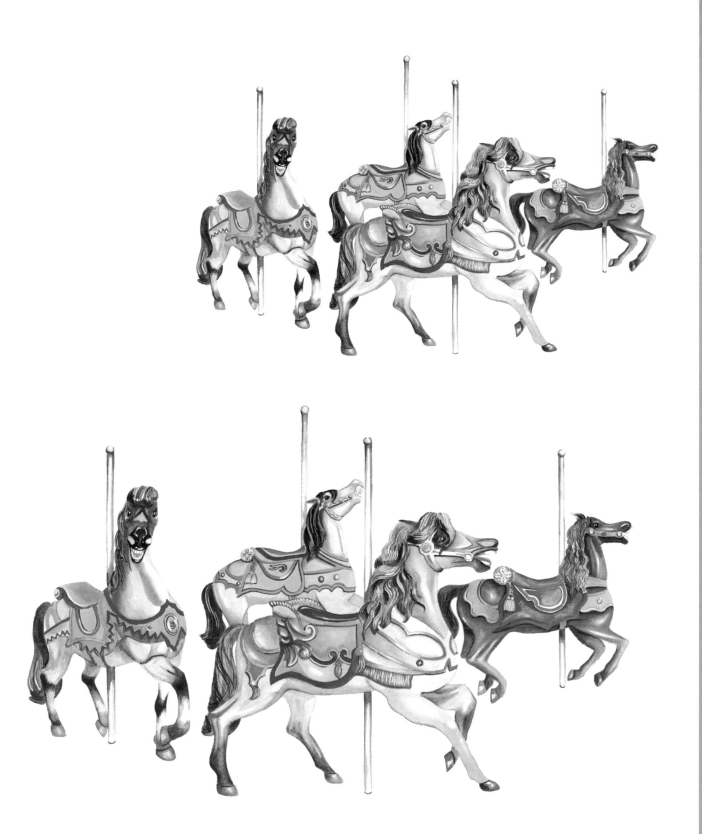

There are many fairs and parks in New Hampshire that have merry-go-rounds, also called carousels. Two carousels—one at Canobie Lake Park and one at Story Land—were built in the nineteenth century. The unusual antique horses and menagerie animals at Canobie Lake are hand-carved and among the finest in the world. Story Land's rare German-made carousel is one of a kind. Its horses rock back and forth and they go around clockwise (most merry-go-rounds turn the other way).

The Deerfield Fair is the oldest family fair in New England and there are many things to do and see. Rides. Contests. Booths with all sorts of games to play and crafts to buy. Be sure not to miss the 4-H activities where boys and girls show their prize animals. Children from the New Hampshire Work Goat Club participate in obstacle races. And New Hampshire's young teamsters show their matched pairs of working steers. In the winter, some of their teams volunteer to haul sleds loaded with maple sap out of the woods.

twenty
20

Just because it's winter and the lakes are frozen solid doesn't mean you can't go fishing! Ice fishing, that is. You and your friends will bring an auger, or drill, to make a hole in the ice and "tip-ups" with red flags that pop up when you've caught a fish. Then you'll need a sled to pull your gear, waterproof boots, warm pants and a jacket, gloves, and your favorite hat. Oh yes, and lots of snacks and a thermos of hot chocolate!

Some people do their ice fishing from inside one of the bobhouses that are clustered out on the ice like little villages. Bobhouses have chairs to sit on while you keep an eye on that hole in the ice, and there's even a stove to keep you warm.

The biggest nonprofit ice-fishing derby in the United States is the Meredith Rotary Fishing Derby, which takes place each year in February on Lake Winnepesaukee.

thirty
30

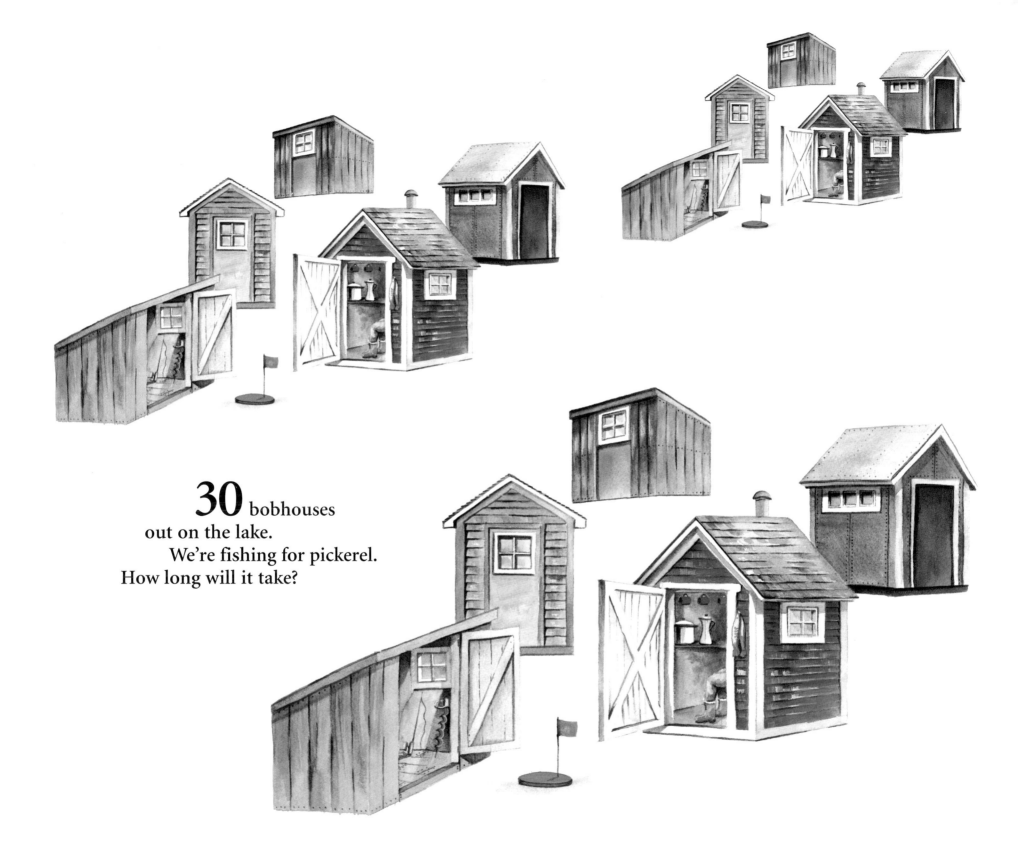

30 bobhouses
out on the lake.
We're fishing for pickerel.
How long will it take?

In the last days of February, when the days are bright and sunny, the nights are cold, and there's still snow in the woods, the maple sap begins to run. During the day the warm sun pulls sap up the maple trunk into its branches. As night cools the air, the sap falls back down. At maple sugaring time we divert some of this sap into buckets to make syrup.

To collect sap for maple syrup, first we drill a hole into the maple tree (but don't worry, the tree heals itself up easily). Then we put a spile or "tap" into the hole. The spile has a hook on which we hang a bucket. Then drip, drip, drip, the sap falls into the bucket. When the buckets are full, we pour the sap into a big barrel and then put the sap buckets back on the trees. Finally, we boil the sap in a big pan over a roaring fire, stirring often so it doesn't burn, and soon the clear liquid thickens into golden syrup. The building where sap is boiled is called a sugar shack. It takes 40 gallons of sap to make one gallon of syrup!

forty
40

40 tin buckets,
one on each tap.
Soon we'll make syrup
from sweet maple sap.

50 sleek cycles
out for a ride,
smooth as the wind
in the spring countryside.

Laconia Motorcycle Week is the oldest national rally in the country. It began in 1916 when people rode their motorcycles in groups from Boston up to the Lakes Region to enjoy our beautiful scenery. In those days the roads were so narrow and bumpy it took a whole day to get here! At first this adventure was called "The Gypsy Tour." Soon the name was changed to Motorcycle Week. You can see beautiful motorcycles of every kind—including big fancy ones called "riding bikes."

There arc many activities during the week, from daily "gypsy tours" all over New Hampshire to racing and even a "Ride to the Sky" up the steep and winding Mt. Washington Auto Road. Imagine thousands of motorcyclists riding all the way to the top! And then back down!

fifty
50

The Karner Blue is our state butterfly. It is an endangered species. In New Hampshire, 50 acres of the butterflies' favorite habitat—pitch pine forest and wild lupine flowers—has been restored to provide a safe place for the butterflies. Other species that benefit from this new home in the Concord Pine Barrens are the Frosted Elfin butterfly and the Duskywing Skipper.

sixty
60

60 blue butterflies
hovering 'round:
      a garden of wings
floats near the ground.

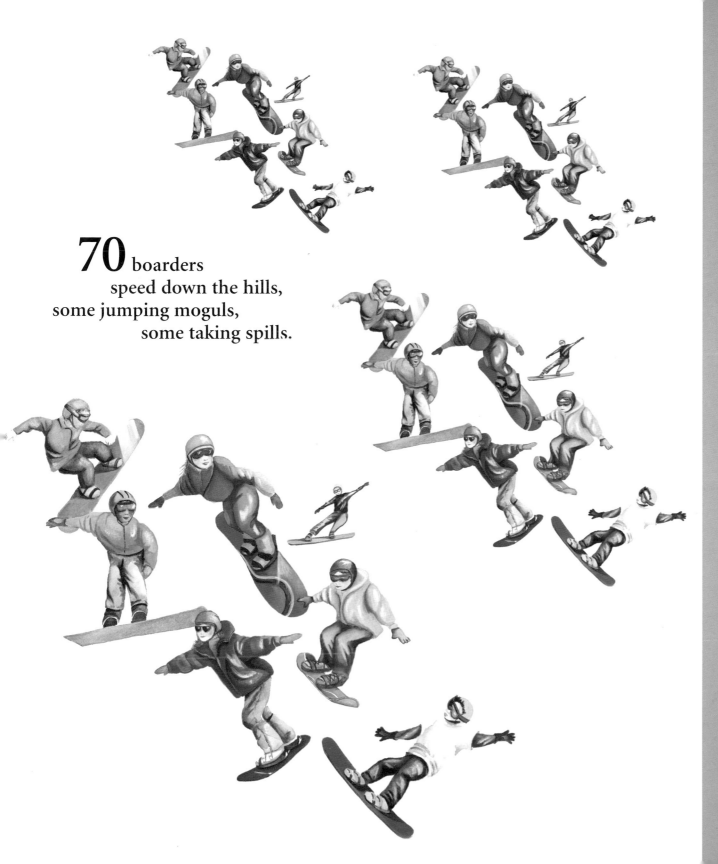

70 boarders
speed down the hills,
some jumping moguls,
some taking spills.

In New Hampshire there are mountains and hills, large and small, where you can have fun in the winter. You can go up as high as you want. Here are some of the ways to get up: rope tows, T-bars, J-bars, chairlifts, gondolas. You can go down as fast as you want. Here are some of the ways to go down: on skis, snowboards, sleds, toboggans...even on your bottom!

Some skiers race down the hill, zigzagging between poles. This kind of race is called a slalom. The first slalom race in the United States was held at Dartmouth College in 1923. The first giant slalom race was held in Tuckerman Ravine in 1937.

Snowboarding is winter's newest sport!

seventy
70

The Abenaki were the first people in what is now New Hampshire and the northeastern part of North America. They carved wampum from the beautiful white and purple quahog shells. Wampum was very valuable and the beads with the most purple in them were the most prized. It was used to make jewelry as well as for payments and presents of all kinds. Pictures, called pictographs, were woven with thousands of shells into wampum belts, which told the Abenaki stories and history and were kept by the Abenaki nation for use in political and religious ceremonies.

Early wampum beads were hand cut for stringing. In the 1700s the Dutch introduced a "wampum drill" that made round holes in the shells.

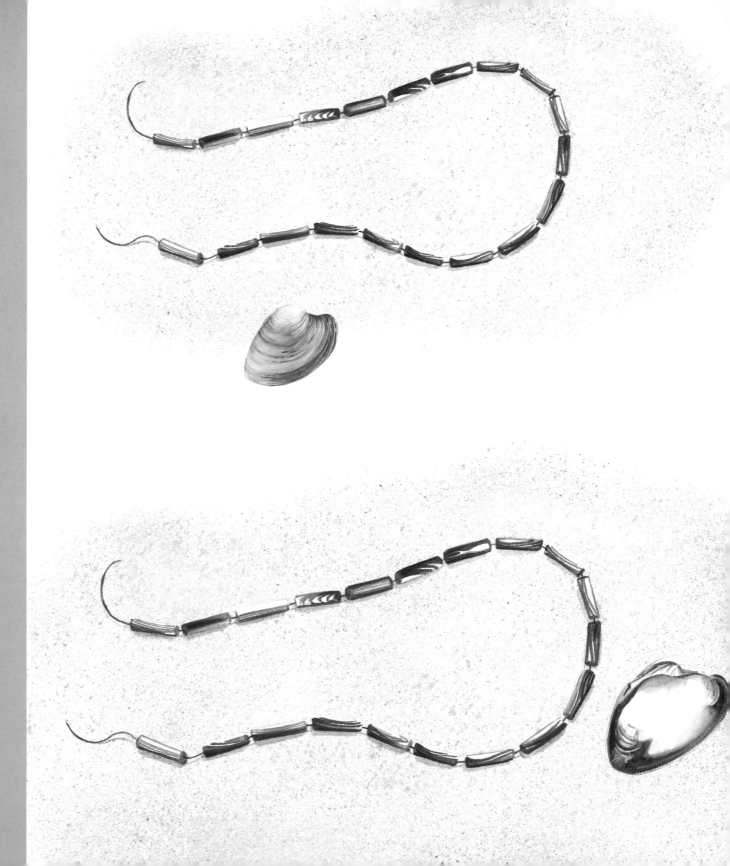

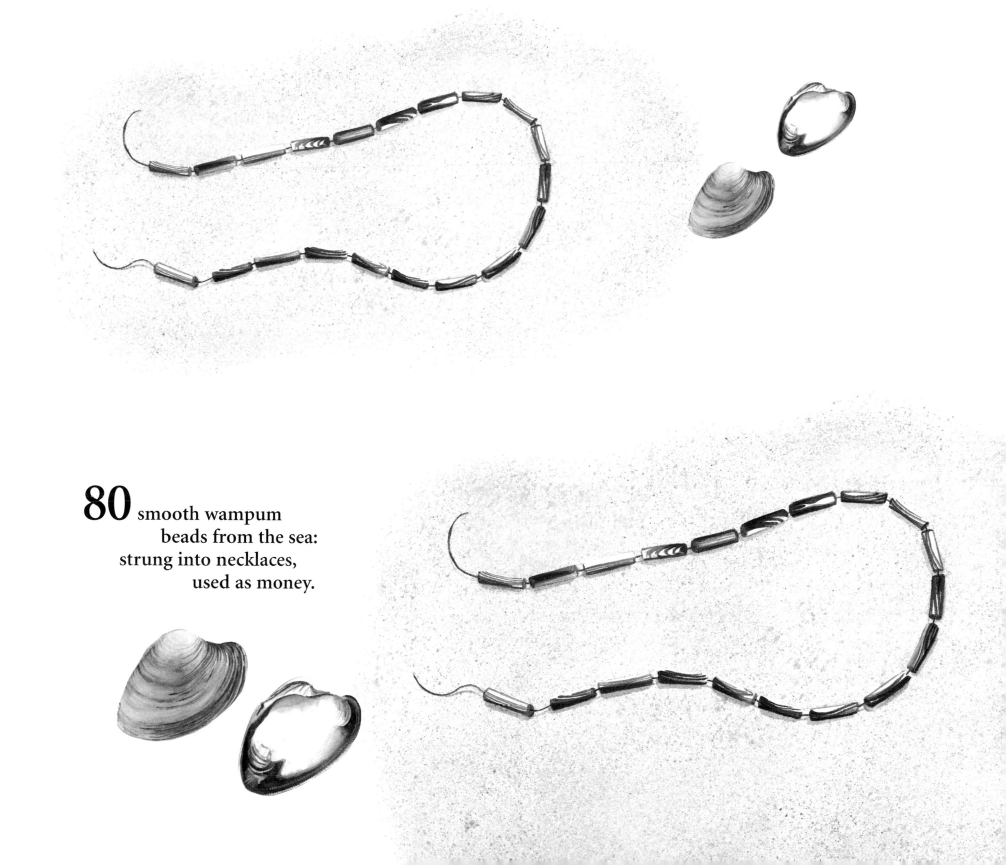

80 smooth wampum
beads from the sea:
strung into necklaces,
used as money.

Apple orchards abound in New Hampshire. More than 90 varieties of apples are grown here. There are at least four varieties of apple that originate in New Hampshire:

the Kearsarge, named after a famous New Hampshire mountain;
the Hampshire, for eating and cooking;
the Granite Beauty, perfect for applesauce; and
the Nodhead with its nut-like flavor.

The Hampshire apple was a "foundling," patented by the Leadbeaters of Gould Hill Farm in 1995.

Apples can be stored in a cold cellar over the winter and brought upstairs to eat or make jellies and pies. There are many orchards in New Hampshire where you can go to pick apples and see apple cider being pressed. You can taste it, too!

ninety
90

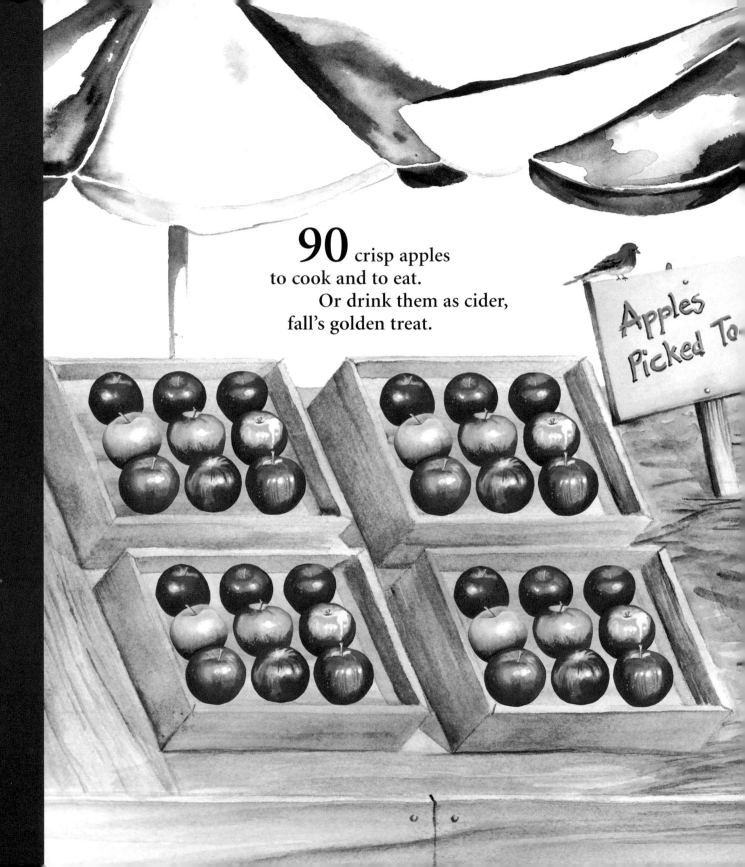

90 crisp apples
to cook and to eat.
Or drink them as cider,
fall's golden treat.

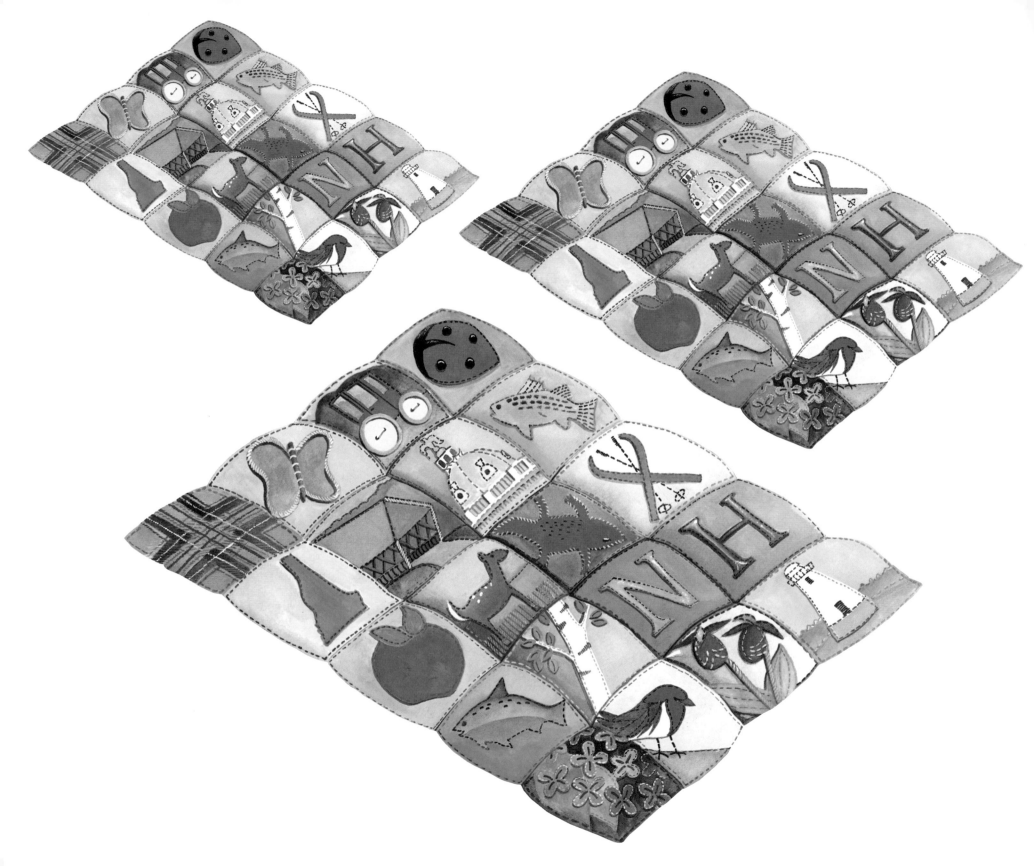

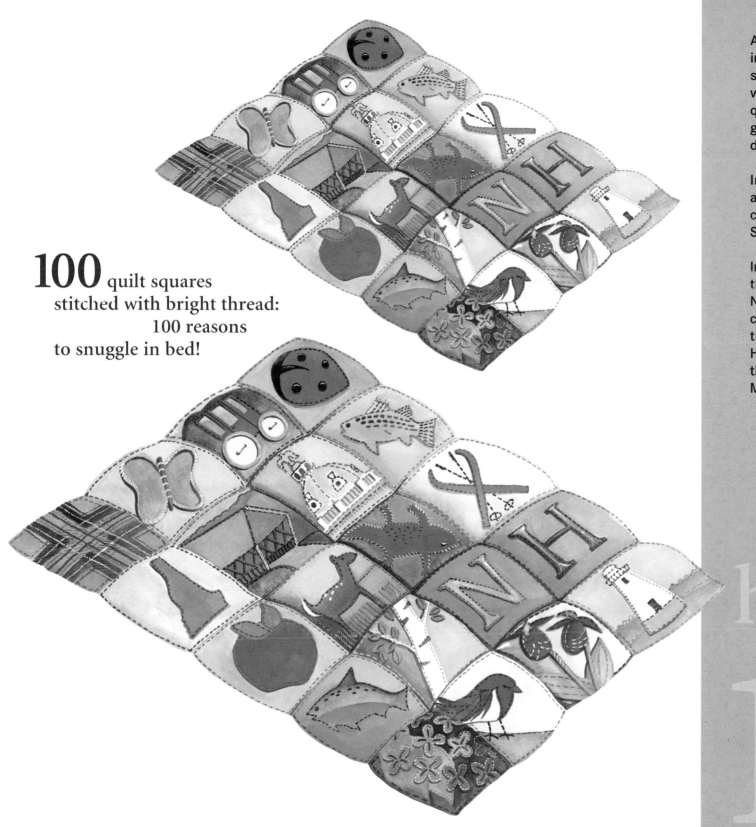

100 quilt squares
stitched with bright thread:
100 reasons
to snuggle in bed!

A project called ABC Quilts was started in New Hampshire in 1988 to bring extra special love and comfort to babies born with dangerous illnesses. Now volunteer quilters of all ages, from grandmothers to grade school children, sew quilts that are delivered to sick babies all over the world.

In 2002, in celebration of the 100th anniversary of 4-H, New Hampshire children presented Governor Jeanne Shaheen with a centennial quilt.

In 1931 Governor John Winant established the League of Arts and Crafts, making New Hampshire the first state in the country to support crafts. This organization is now called the League of New Hampshire Craftsmen and every year they hold a weeklong fair in August at Mt. Sunapee State Park.

one
hundred
100

Marie Harris

Marie Harris has been writing poems and stories since she was eight years old. She and her photographer husband, Charter Weeks, live in the woods in a house they built by hand. In the winter they keep warm with woodstoves. In the summer they tend a vegetable garden, swim in their pond, and go sailing on the ocean in a boat named *Sensei*. They have three sons—Bill, Sebastian, and Manny—who are writers and painters, and five grandchildren.

Marie was New Hampshire's Poet Laureate from 1999 to 2004 and she is the author of *G is for Granite: A New Hampshire Alphabet* as well as four books of poetry, including *Weasel in the Turkey Pen* and *Your Sun, Manny: A Prose Poem Memoir*.

Karen Busch Holman

Karen Holman was born in Montreal, Canada, but her family soon moved to the New England area. Although painting since the age of 10, her first career focused on founding an interior architectural firm with offices in New York City and New Jersey in the 1980s. Her passion for art was much stronger, however, and she "gave it all up" in 1990 to focus on a career in art through graphic design and commercial illustration.

She has continued to share her love of art by teaching children in private art lessons and visiting elementary schools in New Hampshire, teaching children about illustration and art as a career.